BALL
SPORT
TRIVIA

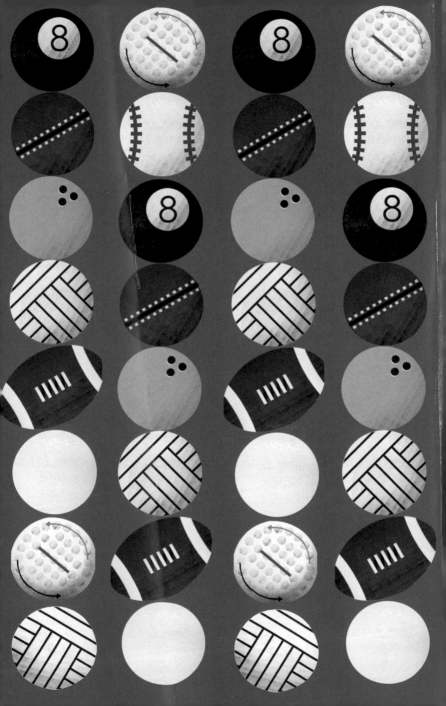

BALL
SPORT
TRIVIA

Over 250 amazing ball-related
facts from the world of sport

ALF ALDERSON

DOG 'n' BONE

Published in 2016 by Dog 'n' Bone Books
An imprint of Ryland Peters & Small Ltd

20–21 Jockey's Fields
London WC1R 4BW

341 E 116th St
New York, NY 10029

www.rylandpeters.com

10 9 8 7 6 5 4 3 2 1

A CIP catalog record for this book is available from
the Library of Congress and the British Library.

ISBN: 978 1 909313 97 2

Printed in China

Editor: Marion Paull
Designer: Jerry Goldie
Illustrator: Blair Frame

CONTENTS

INTRODUCTION

It's a dark, cold winter night and a group of mates are, sensibly, sitting in a warm pub and discussing sport. Apropos of nothing, someone suddenly enquires, "Why are tennis balls fuzzy? And green?"

A second voice pipes up, "Yeah, and what about rugby balls—just why *are* they oval?"*

All very sound questions, but no one has an answer to any of them.

Then it's suggested that as the only journalist among the assembled throng, I should make it my job to search out and discover these facts and more about sports balls.

Well, if you think about it, we pretty much take it for granted that a football, a cricket ball, a baseball or any other sports ball for that matter is the shape it is, and that's that.

Yet what the *Oxford English Dictionary* defines as a "solid or hollow spherical or egg-shaped object that is kicked, thrown, or hit in a game" can be as fundamental a part of life for some people as the change in the seasons.

When a major sporting event such as the World Cup, Super Bowl, Wimbledon, the Masters, the World Series, or the Ashes is under way, life pretty much stops for some of us as we take time off work, skip school, or stay up late to watch a ball hit the back of a net, sail between the posts, or cross a boundary.

So it seems only decent to take a moment or two to consider the history of, and reasons behind, why your favorite sport uses a round or oval ball, a small or large ball, or a heavy or light ball.

For true believers, what Liverpool FC manager Bill Shankly famously said of football/soccer could be applied to most ball sports: *"Some people believe football is a matter of life and death ... It is much, much more important than that"*. I wouldn't perhaps go that far, but they're certainly far from being just a load of balls ...

*Actually, rugby balls are not oval—they're prolate spheres (see page 96)

1

AMERICAN FOOTBALL

> "The word 'genius' isn't applicable in football. A genius is a guy like Norman Einstein."

JOE THEISMANN Sports analyst and former NFL quarterback

ODD BALLS

In the 1905 season, 19 players were killed and 150 seriously injured. President Theodore Roosevelt threatened to close the game down unless it was made safer.

According to declassified CIA records, Hitler's rallying cry "Sieg Heil!", meaning "Hail Victory", was modeled on the techniques used by American football cheerleaders.

Twelve new footballs, sealed in a special box and shipped by the manufacturer, are opened in the officials' locker room two hours prior to the start of an NFL game. These balls are marked with the letter "K" and used exclusively for kicking.

It takes about 3,000 cows to supply enough leather for a year's worth of footballs used by the NFL.

If you applied for a
Green Bay Packers' season ticket
today, you'd have to wait almost
1,000 years before
receiving one.

Since 1941, the official supplier of balls
to the NFL has been Wilson, the world's
biggest manufacturer of American footballs.

Wilson produce some 4,000 balls per day, many by
hand. Their Duke model has been used in every
NFL game for 75 years.

According to a study in *The Wall Street Journal*,
a standard NFL game on TV features just
10 minutes and 43 seconds of action,
while commercials account for another
60 minutes or so of the three-hour game.

The average lifespan for an NFL player
in 1994 was 55 years compared
with 77.6 years for the rest of the
US population.

During the 1958 NFL Championship game, a National Broadcasting Company (NBC) employee ran onto the field, posing as a fan, in order to delay the game, because the national television feed went dead.

MOB RULE

In Jamestown, Virginia, "football" games in the early seventeenth century were similar to the various mob football games played in Britain, using a rudimentary ball made from an inflated pig's bladder.

In the early nineteenth century, students in universities such as Yale, Harvard, Princeton, and Dartmouth played with a ball similar to a British rugby ball. These games were spectacularly violent—so much so that Yale and Harvard banned them for a time in the 1860s.

In 1876 a set of rules was drawn up based on those of rugby union, and the Intercollegiate Football Association was formed. In the 1880s Walter Camp, the "father of American football" introduced various new rules that differentiated the game from rugby.

GET A GRIP

By the mid-nineteenth century, balls were being manufactured in a consistent shape, which made both kicking and handling easier.

In 1934 the circumference of the ball was set at its current size in order to make it easier to grip and throw, but other than improvements in the actual manufacturing process, the way an American football is made has changed relatively little in decades.

NFL football fields must be built facing north/south or in the shade, so that the sun doesn't interfere with play.

"You have to play this game like somebody just hit your mother with a two-by-four."

DAN BIRDWELL former NFL player

> "Most football players are temperamental. That's 90 percent temper and 10 percent mental."

DOUG PLANK NFL football coach

WHAT'S BROWN AND STICKY AND COMES FROM COWS?

The best American footballs are made from brown, tanned cowhide with various forms of weatherproofing and a "pebble grip" texture or tanning to provide a tacky grip.

The white stripes at either end of the ball are designed to improve grip. On top-quality balls they are stitched on rather than painted.

NFL players have been
fined up to $5,000 for
giving a game ball
to a fan.

BALL CONSTRUCTION

In terms of construction, an American football
consists of four panels that are stitched together,
two of them being perforated along adjoining edges
to allow for lacing. One of these two panels has an
additional, reinforced perforation to hold the ball's
inflation valve. An interior, multi-layer lining is
attached to each panel to provide better shape and
durability, and the panels are stitched together
inside out, leaving the lacing hole, through which
the panels are pushed after stitching to turn the ball
right-side out. A three-ply polyurethane bladder
is inserted through the lacing hole to improve air
retention and moisture control.

The last process is inserting the laces, which are
important for obtaining a good grip when holding
and throwing, and may be made of leather or
polyvinyl chloride (PVC).

HARDER, BETTER, FASTER, LONGER

The tackles regularly taken by American football players are some of the hardest in sport. A study by Virginia Tech revealed that players regularly receive hits of over 100Gs, sometimes reaching 150Gs—more than enough to knock the ball out of a player's hand. To give you a comparative force, a slap on the back is usually around 4Gs.

In 1940, the Chicago Bears beat the Washington Redskins 73–0, recording the biggest ever winning margin in an NFL game. The Redskins restored some pride 16 years later, when they defeated the New York Giants 72–41 in the highest scoring NFL game of all time.

The fastest NFL player ever to take to the field game was Dallas Cowboys wide receiver Robert "Bullet Bob" Hayes. Not only did he dominate on the football field but also on the track, where he won the 100 meters at the 1964 Summer Olympics, setting a new world record of 10.06 seconds in the process.

The longest successful field goal in an NFL game is by Matt Prater of the Denver Broncos, who hoofed the ball 64 yards. In 2015 a video surfaced of a Texas Longhorns practice session, where kicker Nick Rose made an 80-yard field goal look easy.

② BASEBALL

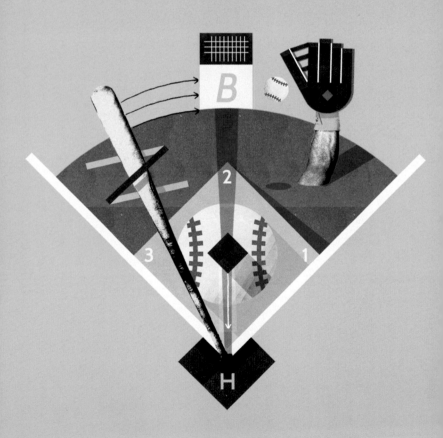

> "Baseball, it is said,
> is only a game. True.
> And the Grand Canyon is
> only a hole in Arizona.
> Not all holes, or games,
> are created equal."

GEORGE WILL US newspaper columnist

ODD BALLS

Before World War Two, baseball enjoyed some popularity in the UK. Many English football/soccer teams shared their grounds with baseball teams, which is why Derby County's former home was known as the Baseball Ground. In 1938, the Great Britain national team even managed to defeat the United States in the Amateur World Series.

All Major League Baseball (MLB) umpires must wear black underwear in case their pants split.

John Smoltz, a pitcher for the Atlanta Braves, burned his chest in 1990 while ironing a shirt that he was wearing.

A curve ball can curve up to 17½in (44.5cm) in the course of being pitched, travels at between 70 and 80 mph (110 and 130 km/h), and rotates at 1900rpm.

Baseball is closely related to the English schoolgirls' game of rounders—at least according to an article written in 1905 by US sports journalist and Baseball Hall of Famer Henry Chadwick, although some aspects, such as the box score, are derived directly from cricket.

SPALDING'S CALL

From 1871 to 1875, A.G. Spalding, the 'inventor' of the baseball as we know it today, pitched every game with a baseball he had developed himself. He won 241 out of 301 games, went on to be inducted in the Baseball Hall of Fame, and for the next 100 years his baseball was the official ball of the US Major Leagues.

Over his career with Boston Red Stockings and Chicago White Stockings, Spalding achieved a 0.323 batting average, an earned-run average of 2.14, and an overall winning percentage of 0.796, a record that still stands today.

"I can wear a baseball cap; I am entitled to wear a baseball cap. I am genetically pre-disposed to wear a baseball cap, whereas most English people look wrong in a baseball cap."

BILL BRYSON author

> "There are three types of baseball players: Those who make it happen, those who watch it happen, and those who wonder what happens."
>
> **TOMMY LASORDA** former Major League player

MATERIAL THINGS

According to the website for MLB (Major League Baseball), the ball 'shall be a sphere formed by yarn wound around a small core of cork, rubber, or similar material, covered with two stripes of white horsehide or cowhide, tightly stitched together,' a basic design that has changed remarkably little from the early baseballs invented by A.G. Spalding.

The MBL (Metro Baseball League) balls made today by Rawlings are still made from leather and have raised seams (with a regulation 108 stitches), a design that has been much the same for over 80 years.

"Half this game is 90 percent mental."

DANNY OZARK former Major League coach and manager

DEADBALL

Prior to 1872, when the dimensions and materials for baseballs were established, baseballs were made by hand from a string-wrapped rubber core with a horsehide cover, and varied from golf ball to softball size, and in weight from 3–6oz (85–170g). These early balls were renowned for their "deadball" feel in play, yet this was still a problem when the balls were standardized in 1872. This early period in baseball's history was known as the "Deadball Era" and home runs were a rarity due to the lack of response from the ball when whacked.

In 1910 George Reach of Reach Sporting Goods invented a baseball with a cork center, which was much more responsive. These balls were secretly used in the 1910 World Series (named after the *New York World* newspaper according to some; as a result of American hubris according to others) and with them the number of home runs increased, leading to cork balls becoming the standard for Major League Baseball in 1911.

During World War Two, the US military developed the T-13 Beano hand grenade, which was designed to the same specifications as a baseball. The thinking behind this was that every American man should be familiar with throwing a baseball, therefore encouraging more accurate throwing by soldiers.

"Major League Baseball has asked its players to stop tossing baseballs into the stands during games, because they say fans fight over them and they get hurt. In fact, the Florida Marlins said that's why they never hit any home runs. It's a safety issue."

JAY LENO
comedian, writer, producer, and TV host

SMALL CHANGES

Pitchers developed new styles of deliveries to take full advantage of the more responsive ball. "Scuffballs," for instance, involved the pitcher rubbing a smooth spot on the ball, which caused it both to spin and travel more quickly. It's now banned due to the potential danger to the batter.

White balls became more common as they were easier for the batter to see and hit, which led to an increase in the number of runs being scored. To even things out, a 1931 change favored pitchers. A thin layer of rubber was wrapped around the cork core and the seams were raised. These changes deadened the ball slightly and the raised seams allowed pitchers to get a better grip to impart more rotation to the ball.

The number of balls used in a game from the 1920s onward could be between 20 and 60, because it became the fashion for fans to keep foul balls as souvenirs, instead of handing them in for free admission to another game. Also, umpires would remove dirty, worn, or scuffed balls from play much sooner than they had done previously.

- O - X - O - X - O - X - O -

> "Baseball is very big with my people. It figures. It's the only way we can get to shake a bat at a white man without starting a riot."

DICK GREGORY
African-American comedian, writer, and civil rights activist

No more noticeable changes took place in the design of the ball until Spalding, then the world's major manufacturer of baseballs and official supplier to the MLB, changed from cowhide to horsehide covers in 1974 for economic reasons.

Today the average number of baseballs used per game is 120, with the average life span of a ball being five to seven pitches. The 30 MLB teams get through more than 900,000 balls each season, which costs somewhere in the order of $5.5 million per year (less than the average salary of a New York Yankees player).

> "If it wasn't for baseball, I'd be in either the penitentiary or the cemetery."

BABE RUTH former Major League player

3

BASKETBALL

> "I'm tired of hearing about money, money, money, money, money. I just want to play the game, drink Pepsi, wear Reebok."

SHAQUILLE O'NEAL
Former NBA pro turned TV pundit

ODD BALLS

The smallest ever NBA (National Basketball Association) player was Muggsy Bogues at 5ft 3in, who played for the Washington Bullets in the 1980s.

The tallest was Romania's Gheorghe Mureşan at 7ft 7in, who also played for the Washington Bullets but in the 1990s.

Detroit Pistons' Isiah Thomas scored 16 points in 94 seconds against the New York Knicks in the 1984 NBA playoffs to force the game into overtime—and his team still lost.

The first professional basketball game was played in Toronto, Canada, in 1946.

In 1992, two legendary MJs, Michaels Jackson and Jordan, appeared together in the music video for the King of Pop's single, *Jam*. A basketball that featured in the video was signed by the pair and in 2010 was auctioned for a staggering $294,000. Jordan-related memorabilia is in high demand. In 1992, McDonalds released a limited-edition burger imaginatively titled the McJordan. A bottle of McJordan BBQ sauce was sold at auction for $9,995, 20 years later.

Early basketballs were brown. Orange balls appeared in the 1950s and orange is still the official color for NBA balls. Other leagues use a variety of colors as well as multicolored basketballs.

Just two of the original NBA teams still exist today—the Boston Celtics and the New York Knicks. Every other original team has either folded or moved since the league started.

"Hockey is a sport for white men. Basketball is a sport for black men. Golf is a sport for white men dressed like black pimps."

TIGER WOODS professional golfer

> "If I weren't earning $3 million a year to dunk a basketball, most people on the street would run in the other direction if they saw me coming."

CHARLES BARKLEY
Former NBA pro turned TV pundit

LEATHER FOR CHOICE

Early basketballs were made from four panels of leather stitched together with a rubber bladder inside. A cloth lining was added to the leather for support and uniformity, and, unlike modern balls, they had lacing. This was eventually abandoned in 1937, by which time basketball had become an Olympic sport, having been introduced the previous year in Berlin.

In 1970 the NBA adopted eight rather than four-panel balls as the official ball, while in 1972 Spalding produced the first synthetic leather ball. But in 1983, the company's full-grain leather ball became the NBA's new official ball.

A PEACH OF AN IDEA

Despite being as American as apple pie, basketball was, in fact, invented by a Canadian, James Naismith, in 1891. Naismith was in charge of physical education at Springfield College, Massachusetts, and was looking for an indoor sport to play during the cold winter months.

Naismith's first version involved lobbing a soccer ball into an old peach basket. By 1893 peach baskets had been replaced by iron hoops and hammock-style baskets so that the referee didn't have to climb a ladder and remove the ball after every score.

The change to the basket wasn't the only amendment to Naismith's original rules. The first draft stated that there were nine players on each team and a "player cannot run with the ball" and "must throw it from the spot on which he catches it." In 2010, the first copy of the rules was bought by philanthropist David Booth for $4,338,500.

In 1894, at Naismith's behest, the first purpose-made basketballs were developed by the Spalding Sporting Goods Company. Spalding benefitted enormously from being there at the start, because when the official rules of the game were drawn up, they contained the phrase "… the ball made by A.G. Spalding & Bros. shall be the official ball," which holds to this day.

BOUNCY, BOUNCY

In the nineties, basketballs with a textured pebble surface were introduced. These gave better contact between the player's finger pads and the ball, so that passing and shooting became more accurate, as well as making it easier to impart spin to the ball.

Today, a standard 29½in (75cm) basketball has about 4,118 "pebbles" on its outer surface, and the pebbles have a diameter of a tenth of an inch (2.5mm).

Another major innovation came in 2001, when Spalding produced the Infusion ball, which had a built-in pump; and then in 2005 came the Never Flat, which the company guaranteed would have a consistent bounce for at least a year.

Not all innovations have been well received, however. In January 2006, the NBA introduced yet another new official ball, Spalding's Cross Traxxion, but players claimed that it was slippery, hard to hold, and the ball's increased friction cut their hands. In addition, the new ball bounced an average of 4in (10cm) less than the old leather ball, as well as absorbing moisture more slowly.

Cross Traxxion lasted just one season before the NBA went back to a traditional leather ball. The current Spalding Official Game NBA Basketball has a top-grade, full-grain Horween leather cover and retails for $169.99. And it's orange ...

HE SHOOTS, HE SCORES

The record for the longest basketball shot is 415ft (126.5m). The feat, by YouTubers How Ridiculous, was achieved by throwing the ball from the side of Australia's Gordon Dam into a net positioned on the ground below.

On November 12, 2015, players from the Harlem Globetrotters broke three world records for throwing a basketball into the hoop. Firstly, Thunder Law broke the record for a blindfolded shot by sinking a 69-ft, 6-in (21.2-m) jumper. Next, Handles Franklin nailed a 60-ft, 7-in (18.5-m) throw to break the record for the furthest shot while kneeling down. Finally, Big Easy Lofton hit a 50-ft, 3-in (15.3-m) basket to claim the record for the longest hook shot.

CURRENT BALLS

Leather remains one of the main materials of choice for the outer panels, although the molded rubber composite basketball was introduced in 1942. This had the advantages of being cheaper to produce and less prone to wear and tear, especially when used on rough outdoor surfaces.

Balls are generally designated for either indoor or all-surface use. Indoor-use balls are made of leather or absorbent composites and all-surface ones, known as indoor/outdoor balls, are made of rubber or durable composites.

Major basketball manufacturers besides Spalding include Rawlings, who have produced basketballs since 1902 and make a 10-panel ball known as the TEN; Wilson, who produce the official NCAA game ball; and Molten, a Japanese company who provide the International Basketball Federation (FIBA) and the Olympic Games with their official balls.

Indoor balls are generally more expensive than all-surface ones, and may have to be broken in first to scuff up the surface for better grip when in play.

4

CUE SPORTS

> "For those viewers watching in black and white, the pink ball is just behind the green."

TED LOWE snooker commentator

ODD BALLS

A cue ball accelerates from zero to 30 mph (48 km/h) in a fraction of a second when hit, and can generate friction temperatures of up to 482°F (250°C) between the ball and the table cloth.

Players in championship billiard games may walk up to three miles (5km) while circling the table and moving from the table to their chair.

Belgian company Saluc (see page 37) supply 80 percent of the world's billiard balls. The company started making balls in the 1960s and now exports over 99 percent of its production to more than 60 countries.

Phenolic resin billiard balls require a minimum five-ton load to reach breaking point.

> "All the reds are in the open now apart from the blue."

JOHN VIRGO
former professional snooker player turned commentator

Cue balls on coin-operated pool machines are either bigger (known as a "grapefruit") or denser (known as a "rock") than regular pool balls in order to allow the return mechanism to differentiate it from the "object" balls. Newer tables use a magnetic ball that is of regulation, or very near to regulation, size because this plays better than heavier or oversized balls.

The oldest popular forms of cue games are English billiards and carom billiards, which date back to the fifteenth century. Similar games can be found worldwide, such as the Asian game *yotsudama*, which literally means "four balls," and the Finnish game *kaisa*, which uses 15 numbered all-white balls.

> "I know people say Ronnie O'Sullivan is the best thing in snooker since Tiger Woods."

WILLIE THORNE
former professional snooker player turned commentator

IVORY BALLS

By the nineteenth century, the composition of the balls had moved on from their original materials of wood or clay—which did not have a consistent size, shape, weight, or density—to ivory. The ivory had to be seasoned for up to two years before being made into balls.

Elephant tusks vary in density, which led to inconsistencies in weight and mass, and it was possible to make a maximum of just eight balls from one tusk. The best balls came from the small tusks of female elephants.

By the beginning of the twentieth century, up to 12,000 animals a year were killed to supply the British game.

CUE THE CONFUSION

The difference between billiards, pool, and snooker is a bit of a minefield. A simplified explanation is that billiards covers all games involving a cue and round balls that can be played on a billiard table—some tables have pockets, some don't. Pool refers to games that are played on a six-pocket billiard table. The aim is to hit the cue ball and pocket certain balls on the table before your opponent. Snooker also involves six pockets, but is played on a much larger table than pool. Each snooker ball has a points value when potted. To win, a player must build up a score that's higher than an opponent's total.

EXPLOSIVE DEVELOPMENT

Luckily for elephants, in 1869 inventor John Wesley Hyatt developed the cellulose nitrate billiard ball. However, although it provided balls with a consistent shape, size, and density, celluloid occasionally exploded in the production process.

The problem of exploding balls was overcome by using plastic compounds, such as Bakelite and Crystalate, and by the late 1920s plastic composite balls became common. They were used in the British amateur billiards championships from 1926 and in the professional game from 1929.

SNOOKERED

Snooker, which has its origins in table ball games played by British Army officers in India, gradually became as popular as billiards until by the 1930s it overtook billiards in popularity.

Originally known as "black pool," snooker was first played using 15 red balls and one black, with the eventual addition of higher-scoring yellow, green, and pink balls, and then later the blue and brown.

The name "snooker" is apparently derived from the slang term for a first-year officer at the Royal Military Academy in Woolwich, London.

Since World War Two, snooker and pool have considerably overshadowed billiards. Pool in particular has become enormously popular since the introduction of coin-operated machines in pubs and clubs.

To practice, pool and snooker players use training balls decorated with various systems of stripes, spots, target rings, or differently colored halves. These allow you to see and develop the effects of topspin, backspin, and sidespin.

BALL IN HAND

Saluc is the only company to manufacture phenolic resin balls, which they do under the name Aramith. These are far more impact- and scratch-resistant than polyester balls, as well as lasting up to five times longer. They are also up to a hundred times finer grained, which allows them to hold their glossy finish and leads to less wear and tear to both balls and table cloth.

Production involves 13 stages over a three-week period, including casting, curing, grinding, and polishing before a final hand check.

Frenzy Sports and the splendidly named Elephant Balls produce polyester and acrylic balls.

5

CRICKET

> # "Cricket civilizes people and creates good gentlemen."

ROBERT MUGABE President of Zimbabwe

ODD BALLS

The characteristics of a cricket ball change during the game. Fast bowlers prefer to play with a new ball since it is harder, travels faster, and bounces more than an older one. Older balls are better for spin bowlers because their rougher surface imparts better spin.

Ball tampering can give bowlers an unfair advantage against batsmen. As a result, the rules of the game instruct that it's forbidden to:

- Rub any substance apart from saliva or sweat onto the ball
- Rub the ball on the ground
- Scuff the ball with any rough object, including fingernails
- Pick at or lift the seam of the ball

Rain stopping play is a common occurrence in cricket, but on rare occasions the animal kingdom likes to throw a spanner in the works, too. In the past, a pig, sparrow, hedgehog, mouse, and a swarm of bees have all managed to halt progress on the pitch.

"Cricket is basically baseball on Valium."

ROBIN WILLIAMS actor and comedian

Shoaib Akhtar of Pakistan, also known as the "Rawalpindi Express," is regarded as the fastest bowler in the history of cricket. He set an official world record with a delivery of 100.2 mph (161.3 km/h) against England in the 2003 World Cup.

How bowling speeds in cricket are classified:

	mph	km/h
Fast (express)	90+	145+
Fast-medium	80–89	129–145
Medium-fast	70–79	113–129
Medium	60–69	97–113
Medium-slow	50–59	80–97
Slow-medium	40–49	64–80
Slow	below 40	below 64

The Hot Spot is an infrared imaging system that allows the umpire to determine where the ball has struck—the infrared image shows a bright spot where contact friction from the ball has elevated the local temperature. It uses two cameras positioned at either end of the ground and measures heat friction generated by the impact of ball on pad, bat, glove, and anywhere else.

Ball Spin RPM has recently been introduced on TV to show the rotation speed of the ball when spin bowlers are in action, or how fast the ball is spinning after release.

PUT A CORK IN IT

The essential ingredients of a modern cricket ball are very utilitarian—a core of cork layered with tightly wound string, which is then covered by a leather case.

Early cricket balls were even more basic. A lump of wood was used in an eighth-century Punjab bat-and-ball game called *gilli-danda*, and a game that involved throwing stones or sheep shit at an opponent, using a tree trunk or gate as a wicket, was played in south-east England shortly after the Norman invasion of 1066.

By the seventeenth century things were more high-tech. Balls were made from leather stuffed with cloth, hair, and feathers, or a mix of cork and wool known as a "quilt." These were made by "quiltwinders" who wound a length of thread around an octagonal piece of cork to make a core for the leather-bound ball.

UNDER OR OVER ...

The first official regulations for the ball's dimensions date back to 1774, around the same time as underarm bowling began to be replaced by faster overarm bowling. The introduction of a standard size and weight for the ball helped both the batsmen and the bowlers since it made the delivery more predictable.

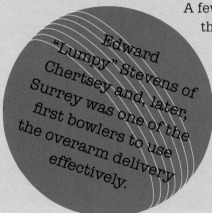

Edward "Lumpy" Stevens of Chertsey and, later, Surrey was one of the first bowlers to use the overarm delivery effectively.

A few years before this, the Duke family from the Eden Valley in Kent started manufacturing the first six-seamed cricket ball, a forerunner of those used in the game today.

SQUEEZE AND SHINE

The cork core used in the balls gave bounce and hardness at the same time as providing enough give to ensure that wooden cricket bats were not damaged. The stitching around the ball was squashed down into a spherical shape with an instrument called, yes, a "squeezer." When the railways arrived, squeezers were often constructed from railway sleeper bolts.

Duke cricket balls are still in production today, and are said to keep their shine longer than other balls. The Duke Special County "A" Grade 1 red cricket ball is used exclusively for Test matches in the UK and first-class county cricket, while the Duke County International "A" is the choice of the majority of ECB (England and Wales Cricket Board) accredited Premier League games.

> "Down the mine I dreamed of cricket; I bowled imaginary balls in the dark; I sent the stumps spinning and heard them rattling in the tunnels."

HAROLD LARWOOD
Nottinghamshire and England fast bowler, and former coal miner

HIGH-TECH BALLS

Australian company Kookaburra was established in the late nineteenth century by English émigré Alfred Grace Thompson. Like all other successful cricket-ball manufacturers, Kookaburra moved from labor-intensive, hand-sewn balls to machine-manufactured products, opening a custom-built plant in Melbourne in 1946 and later developing state-of-the-art machines for cricket-ball production.

A similar path was followed in the UK by Alfred Reader & Company. Reader became one of the largest manufacturers of cricket balls in the UK, and by the 1970s was using high-tech research and development to produce balls made from synthetic cork. Reader worked in partnership with Tiflex Limited from Liskeard in Cornwall, which specializes in research into impact abrasion and vibration-absorbing compounds.

"You might not think that's cricket, and it's not, it's motor racing."

MURRAY WALKER motorsport commentator and journalist

RED OR WHITE?

The outside of a modern cricket ball is made from four separate pieces of leather. Two pairs are sewn together on the inside, forming two halves, and the join in one half is rotated at 90 degrees to the other. A raised seam between these two halves is sewn together with six rows of stitches made from string. The ball is then usually dyed red, but other colored balls, such as orange or yellow, are used for improved visibility, along with white for floodlit matches.

The origin of the traditional deep-red color of cricket balls is disputed, although one explanation is that it may have derived from the pigment reddle (red ocher), which was used to brand sheep.

Interestingly, white balls swing more and deteriorate faster than red balls—the polyurethane coating added to a white ball to prevent it getting dirty is the reason for the extra swing. Some people claim that white balls are harder than red ones, hurt fielders' hands, and can even break bats.

6

CROQUET

"The boys always ganged up on the girls—my croquet balls were constantly being knocked into hedges and flower beds."

PIPPA MIDDLETON describing the tough life of a toff

ODD BALLS

Rapper Sean "Puffy" Combs celebrated his 2008 induction into the Hollywood Walk of Fame with a $2 million croquet party.

The 1988 film *Heathers*, starring Christian Slater and Winona Ryder, introduced the sport of strip croquet.

Wimbledon's famous All England Lawn Tennis and Croquet Club was founded in 1868 as the All England Croquet Club, eventually changing its name when tennis became more popular.

A study by Dr Ian Plummer of Oxford University revealed that on a hot English summer's day the surface temperature of a black croquet ball reached 151.2°F (66.2°C) compared with 119.1°F (48.4°C) for a yellow ball.

MALLETS AND BALLS

Mallet and ball games that involved knocking a wooden ball through a willow hoop were common in medieval Britain and Europe. Later, Samuel Pepys, in his 1661 diaries, comments on a game called "pall-mall", which involved using a mallet to smack a ball down a 1,000-yard (914.5-m) long pitch.

Pepys's pall-mall was played in an area close to the modern-day Pall Mall in London—the street's name appears to have been derived from the game.

Lawn billiards, where players used a mallet to hit a ball through an iron ring fixed to the ground, was popular in Victorian times, but this was eventually superseded by croquet as we know it today.

A French doctor developed a mallet-and-ball game called "croquet" in 1832 as exercise for his patients, while a similar Irish game, "crookey," was introduced to England in the 1850s.

BALLS TO FIT ALL WALLETS

The first standardized croquet balls were made by John Jaques of London, who claim to have invented the sport in 1851. They still make croquet sets, ranging in price from $170 (£129.99) to over $7,000 (£4,999.99).

Jaques's early balls were carved from a single block of Turkish boxwood and had an oil-paint surface, but this surface was replaced in 1906 with a coating called "Glisglos."

A new composite ball—the Eclipse—was introduced by Jaques in 1945. It had a cork, and later a solid plastic, core and a casing that had been dipped in nitrocellulose for additional protection against wear and tear.

ECLIPSE OF THE EMPIRE

The Eclipse had its problems—if crushed, it could chip, crack, or peel, and in hot conditions black balls could occasionally explode. British company Ayres took over the market with its Championship ball, which became a bestseller worldwide, although production stopped after World War Two.

Other companies, including Slazenger and the British Composition Company, moved into the market with composite balls. More recently, Barlow (South Africa), Dawson (Australia), Sunshiny (Taiwan), and Willhoite (USA) have arrived on the scene. Different companies use different production techniques. Dawson balls, for example, are manufactured from polyurethane in a two-piece mold while Barlow use a solid nylon core and casing.

The "roundest" balls are apparently made by Sunshiny or Willhoite. Bounce, measured on six points of the ball, is also important.

A croquet ball is milled, or shaped, in two directions with some 50 cuts each way to give the characteristic textured diamond pattern. This reduces gradually to four small circles, known as poles, on which companies engrave their marks.

HEAVY HITTERS

Winston Churchill was a big fan of the sport and had a croquet lawn at Chartwell, his home in Kent, England.

In the 1940s and 50s, croquet became all the rage among the Hollywood elite, with various studio heads playing regularly.

In Stephen King's horror novel *The Shining*, the main character terrorizes his wife with a croquet mallet, rather than the axe wielded by Jack Nicholson in the film version.

7

FOOTBALL/ SOCCER

> "Some people believe football is a matter of life and death. I am very disappointed with that attitude ... It is much, much more important than that."

BILL SHANKLY
former professional player and manager of Liverpool FC

ODD BALLS

In 1979 a Scottish Cup tie between Falkirk and Inverness Thistle was postponed 29 times because of bad weather.

The Isles of Scilly have two football teams, the Gunners and the Wanderers. They play each other every week in the league, and also meet in cup ties.

The Albanian national team left the UK in disgrace in 1990 after a stopover at Heathrow, where they went on a literal free-for-all in the airport shops, believing that "duty free" meant "help yourself."

Pedro Gatica cycled from Argentina to Mexico for the 1986 World Cup, but couldn't afford to get into the matches, so he set about haggling for a ticket. While doing so his bike was stolen.

Romanian midfielder Ion Radu was sold by second division Jiul Petrosani to Valcea in 1998 for 1,102lb (500kg) of pork.

DODGY DECISIONS

A Brazilian referee left the match where
he'd been officiating on horseback at
a swift gallop after shooting dead a player
who disputed a penalty decision.

Danish referee Henning Erikstrup was officiating
at the Norager versus Ebeltoft league match when,
as he was about to blow for full-time, his dentures
fell out. While he was searching for them, Ebeltoft
leveled the score to 4–4, but despite their protests,
Erikstrup disallowed the goal, popped his teeth
back in, and blew the final whistle.

**When the Football Association was set up in
1863, there was much discussion over Rule X:
"… any player … shall be at liberty to charge,
hold, trip or hack [his opponents]." It was
subsequently dropped.**

"A penalty
is a cowardly way
to score."

PELÉ
former professional player

> **"I spent a lot of money on booze, birds, and fast cars. The rest I just squandered."**
>
> **GEORGE BEST**
> former professional player

KEEP UP

The world keepie-uppie record is held by Dan Magness of England, who kept a regulation football in the air for 26 hours using just his feet, legs, shoulders, and head. He is also the holder of the record for the longest distance traveled while doing keepie-uppie, managing to go 36 miles (48km) without letting the ball touch the ground, and in the process visiting five Premier League grounds in London.

Milene Domingues (a model and former women's footballer, also the ex-wife of striker Ronaldo) holds the record for the longest keepie-uppie if measured by the number of touches accumulated—55,198.

"LOSER DIES"

In South America 3,000 years ago, the Mayans played a form of football using a solid rubber ball weighing up to 20lb (9kg) and some 20in (51cm) in diameter. The losers were often sacrificed to the gods. The Aztecs played a similar "loser dies" game called *tlachtli*.

China's Han Dynasty (206 BC–220 AD) had a game called *tsu chu* (*tsu*, "kicking the ball with feet"; *chu*, "a stuffed ball made of leather") and the Japanese played a football-style game called *kemari* around 2,000 years ago.

In North America, Native Americans were recorded in the early seventeenth century playing a violent game of 500-a-side football called *pasuckuakohowog*.

The Aboriginal people of Australia's modern-day Victoria played a version of football called *marn grook*, while in the Middle Ages Italy had *calcio* and France *soule* or *choule*, both using a stitched leather ball stuffed with leather and bran and deriving from a Roman game called *harpastum*.

HIDE YOUR CHILDREN

Football of sorts has been played in England from the eighth century onward. Games were often played between neighboring towns and villages with hundreds of players kicking nine bells out of each other as well as the ball, which was an inflated pig's bladder encased in leather.

Modern-day examples can be seen in Christmas and Hogmanay games at Kirkwall in the Orkneys and Duns in Berwickshire, and Shrove Tuesday matches at Alnwick, Corfe Castle, and Sedgefield. Shop windows may be boarded up to prevent them being smashed in the melee, and children and small dogs are ushered indoors to safety.

MAKING A BALL OF IT

In 1855 Charles Goodyear designed the first footballs to be made with vulcanized rubber bladders. Prior to this, balls made from pig's bladders were standard.

The ball consisted of 18 sections arranged in six panels of three strips each, with a lace-up slit on one side. The ball case was stitched inside out and then reversed so the stitching was on the inside. A bladder was inserted and inflated through one remaining slit, which was then laced up.

The Football Association officially codified the rules of the game and, in 1872, decided on the weight and dimensions of the ball. To all intents and purposes, these are still in use today in world football.

During the early twentieth century, it was common for footballs to deflate during the course of a match.

The old brown leather balls would soak up moisture and gain considerable weight, and this along with the protruding lacing often resulted in head and neck injuries. As late as the 1970s, West Brom player Jeff Astle and Danny Blanchflower of Spurs both suffered chronic brain injuries as a result of heading heavy footballs, which eventually led to their deaths.

Later, various synthetics were applied to the ball's outer casing to repel water, and a new valve was introduced, which did away with the need to have a laced slit on the ball.

In the 1940s a cloth carcass was inserted between the outer and the bladder to maintain the shape of the ball, as well as providing a certain amount of dampening and additional strength.

White balls were introduced in the 1950s as they were easier to see under floodlights, and orange balls for snowy conditions.

PANEL GAMES

In the 1950s Danish company Select developed the 32-panel ball, which maintained a more spherical shape than the 18-panel version.

Black-and-white footballs were introduced for the 1970 Mexico World Cup, because they were easier to see on TV. The iconic Adidas Telstar ball had 12 black pentagons and 20 white hexagons.

Numerous design improvements since then include the first fully synthetic football, the Adidas Tango Azteca in 1986, and in 2006 the Adidas +Teamgeist, a high-tech, thermally bonded ball made up of 14 panels.

The latest development is the Nike Ordem 3, which has a fuse-welded synthetic leather casing and a geometric 12-panel design plus Aerowtrac grooves, which, say Nike, are "designed to provide an accurate and stable flight by helping ensure a steady flow of air across the ball no matter what speed it is moving at."

All a far cry from a waterlogged leather lump that would deflate as the match progressed …

FOR THE LOVE OF THE GAME?

Much like their battle to be the world's best player, Cristiano Ronaldo and Lionel Messi also duke it out to be the world's highest earning footballer. According to *Forbes* magazine, Ronaldo topped the list in 2015, taking home a cool $79.6 million—that's over $9,000 every hour. Messi is snapping at his heels though, thanks to his $73.8 million paycheck in the same year.

At the opposite end of the pay scale is Kevin Poole. In 2013, English club Burton Albion suffered an injury crisis that left them without a reserve goalkeeper. Luckily, Poole, one of the club coaches, was a former goalkeeper. He agreed to sit on the bench provided Burton Albion paid him with cookies, specifically chocolate Hobnobs.

LONG-RANGE EFFORTS

The world record for the longest goal scored in a professional football match is held by Stoke City goalkeeper Asmir Begović. A mere 13 seconds after kick off against Southampton, Begović cleared a back pass from his defender, hoofing the ball 100 yards (91.9m), past Southampton's keeper Artur Boruc and into the net.

The fastest goal scored in a game is two seconds, when Nawaf Al Abed took a shot after being passed the ball from the kick off. It was the first goal in a 4–0 victory for Al-Hilal against Al-Shoalah in the Saudi league.

RESPECT YOUR ELDERS

At the time of writing, the oldest active professional footballer is Kazuyoshi Miura, who at the age of 49 is a forward for Yokohama FC, a team from Japan's J-League.

The oldest player in English Football League history is Neil McBain, whose career spanned 33 years and seven clubs, including Manchester United and Liverpool. He retired in 1947 at the age of 51 but continued on in the game as a manager.

Older still is Mexican striker Salvador Reyes, the oldest player to participate in a professional game. In 2008, Reyes turned out at the age of 71 for his old club, CD Guadalajara (popularly known as Chivas), kicking the game off and exchanging a few passes before being substituted.

The youngest ever player in a professional match was Mauricio Baldevieso. In 2009, at the age of 12 years, 362 days, Baldevieso played as a striker for Bolivian side Aurora.

Scouting for young talent is a huge part of the modern game, but Belgian club FC Racing Boxberg took things to new extremes when they signed Bryce Brites, a 20-month-old baby.

8
GOLF

> **"If you are caught on a golf course during a storm and are afraid of lightning, hold up a 1-iron. Not even God can hit a 1-iron."**

LEE TREVINO former professional golfer, who was struck by lightning while playing in the Western Open in Chicago in 1975

ODD BALLS

While playing a round in 1899, American Ab Smith produced what he described as a "bird of a shot," and the term "birdie" evolved from there.

The longest recorded drive on an ordinary golf course is 515 yards by Michael Hoke Austin of Los Angeles, California, in the US National Seniors Open Championship at Las Vegas, Nevada on September 25, 1974.

A putt measured at 140ft 2⊡in was sunk on the 18th hole at St Andrews by Bob Cook in the International Fourball Pro Am Tournament on October 1, 1976.

Pro golfer John Hudson scored two consecutive holes-in-one at the 11th and 12th holes (195 yards and 311 yards respectively) in the 1971 Martini Tournament at Norwich, England. The chance of this is 67,000,000:1.

The word "caddy" comes from the French "cadet," meaning "the boy" or "the youngest of the family."

 Annual worldwide production of golf balls: 850 million

The longest hole-in-one is 427 yards at the 16th at Lake Hefner course, Oklahoma City, USA by Lou Kretlow in March 1961.

"What most people don't understand is that UFOs are on a cosmic tourist route. That's why they're always seen in Arizona, Scotland, and New Mexico. Another thing to consider is that all three of those destinations are good places to play golf. So there's possibly some connection between aliens and golf."

ALICE COOPER
singer-songwriter whose brand of hard rock is designed to shock

HAMMERS AND FEATHERS

The first golf balls were made from wood and were used in Scotland in 1550, although there are records of games similar to golf being played in China in the eleventh century and Holland in the thirteenth century.

A ball known as the "featherie" was introduced in Scotland in 1618, so called because it was made from a leather case packed with a "top hat full" of boiled goose or chicken feathers.

The materials were wet during construction so that as they dried out the feathers expanded and the leather contracted. The ball was hammered into a round shape, coated with several layers of paint, and punched with the ball maker's mark to create a hard ball that could be driven hundreds of yards.

80 percent of all golfers will never achieve a handicap of less than 18.

The longest recorded drive of a featherie was 361 yards by Samuel Messieux in 1836 on St Andrews Old Course, although a typical drive was 150–175 yards (compared with 180–250 yards with a modern ball).

Featheries were expensive, as were clubs, so golf was a rich man's sport.

PUT YOUR GUT INTO IT

In 1848 Rev. Dr Robert Adams Paterson of St Andrews introduced the "guttie" ball, which was less expensive than the featherie and could be repaired. It brought more people into the game.

The guttie was made by boiling *gutta-percha*, a rubbery tree sap, until it became soft and could be hand-rolled on a board into the correct size and shape.

A renowned maker of gutties was Allan Robertson of St Andrews, one of the first pro golfers. In 1859 he became the first person to record a round of under 80 on the Old Course at St Andrews.

Gutties with a rough surface were found to have a truer flight and travel farther than other versions, which led to balls being beaten with a sharp-edged hammer. By the 1880s gutties were made in molds that created patterns on the surface—forerunners of the dimpled golf ball.

Rubber companies, such as Dunlop, began to mass-produce golf balls, which pretty much resulted in the end of hand-crafted balls.

HASKELL'S BALL

In 1898 US golfer Coburn Haskell came up with the next major development in golf balls, the rubber-core ball. Produced by rubber company B.F. Goodrich (later famous for their tires), these balls were made from a solid rubber core wrapped in rubber thread and encased in a gutta-percha outer casing. They gave the average golfer a good 20 yards extra length in driving from the tee.

In short order, the rubber-core golf ball went into mass production. In the early 1900s, gutta-percha balls were replaced with balata and in 1905 dimpled golf balls made their first appearance.

KING OF THE SWINGERS

The average speed of a PGA pro's swing is around 113 mph, which should send the ball a little under 300 yards. One of the game's biggest swingers is Bubba Watson. In 2015, his average swing speed was 123.52 mph and average drive distance was 315.2 yards. Compare this with one of the slowest swingers, Ben Crane, who has an average clubhead speed of 104.59 mph and drive distance of 271 yards.

DRAG ARTIST

Dimpled balls travel farther than smooth balls as a result of the turbulence caused by the dimples, which reduces drag.

The size and number of the dimples affects the ball's aerodynamics. There are no rules for how many dimples a ball can have—392 is the average and most have between 300 and 500.

Maximum velocity of a golf ball: 250ft per second

The more dimples, the better the ball's stability in flight, but there's a trade-off. The more dimples, the less space between them, and if this is too narrow, it may shear on impact with either the club or the ground and the ball will scuff.

Most dimples ever on a golf ball: 1,070

A wide variation in ball sizes and weights existed when dimpled balls were introduced, and surprisingly it was not until 1991 that standard dimensions for golf balls were agreed between the two main golfing authorities, the Royal & Ancient in Scotland and the United States Golf Association in the USA.

> "I have a tip that will take five
> strokes off anyone's golf game.
> It's called an eraser."

ARNOLD PALMER former professional golfer

EXPLODING BALLS

B.F. Goodrich returned to the scene in 1906 with a pneumatic golf ball (known to explode in hot conditions), followed by experiments with cores of cork, mercury, and metal among other substances. However, the rubber-core golf ball remained the most popular until Spalding brought out the two-piece Executive ball in the 1970s.

Today there are essentially four different types of golf ball:

- One piece: basic, inexpensive balls made from a solid piece of Surlyn thermoplastic with molded dimples

- Two piece: hard-wearing balls suitable for long driving and popular with recreational golfers. Made with a solid, hard-plastic core of high-energy acrylate or resin covered with tough Surlyn or specialty plastic

- Three piece: made with a core that either contains a gel or liquid (such as sugar and water) or is solid, windings of rubber thread, and a plastic cover

- Four piece: made with a solid rubber core, two inner covers, and a thin but durable urethane outer layer to provide a longer hit and a better feel on the green

9

HANDBALL

"… it's a hybrid version of soccer, water polo, and lacrosse."

TOM FITZGERALD US handball team member

ODD BALLS

The world record attendance for a handball match is 44,189 for a German league game between HSV Hamburg and the Mannheim Rhein-Neckar Lions on September 6, 2014.

Handball was initially an 11-a-side outdoor game. Numbers were eventually reduced to seven-a-side and the game was brought indoors, effectively making it weatherproof.

Former Olympic and World Champion Ivano Balić is often cited as the greatest handball player ever, having been voted World Player of the Year twice in his career and winning five Most Valuable Player (MVP) awards in a row in international competitions.

The largest handball ever made was an huge 5ft, 3in (171cm) in diameter.

WHICH HAND IS IT?

Confusingly, there are at least a dozen versions of handball played around the world. Team handball is the most popular, and the one covered in this chapter, but other versions include:

- **Gaelic handball**: players hit the ball against a wall with their hand instead of a racket

- **American handball**: similar to Gaelic handball, from which it originates

- **Eton Fives**: a handball game played in a few select English public schools

- **Keatsen**: a version of handball from Friesland in the Netherlands played between two teams of three players

STRANGE-SOUNDING NAMES

The ancient Egyptians had a handball game, the ancient Greeks played *urania*, the Romans enjoyed *harpastum* (played with hands and feet), and medieval Germans played *fangballspiel*. All of these involved the use of a ball and hands.

A game in medieval France involved batting the ball with the hands, and similar games are known to have been played by the Inuit of Greenland and in South America.

SCHOOL RULES

The first official rules for the game were introduced in 1898 when Holger Nielsen, a Danish Olympian and schoolmaster, drew up the rules for *håndbold,* based, in turn, on the rules of a local game called *raffball*, which translates as "snatchball."

The idea behind these rules was that fewer school windows would be broken than when playing football, because the players would have more control over the ball.

A second set of rules was developed in Germany and used in the first international handball match between Germany and Austria in 1925.

The game proved so popular that the International Amateur Handball Federation was founded in 1928.

OLYMPIC SPORT

Handball was introduced to the Olympics in 1936 in Berlin at the request of Adolf Hitler. The sport was dropped after this single appearance, and did not appear in the games again until 1972, coincidentally in Germany again, this time in Munich. Women's handball was added to the program at the 1976 Montreal Olympics.

Russian Andrey Lavrov is the only handball player to win three Olympic gold medals.

Team Handball, as played in the Olympic Games, is especially popular in mainland Europe, although it's very much overshadowed by football/soccer. This is despite handball's precursors being among the oldest games in sport—it seems that hitting a ball with the hands is almost as natural as kicking one.

SELECTION PANEL

There are no detailed records of the construction of the balls used in early, rudimentary versions of handball, although evidence from Ireland suggests that an early version of handball played there used a ball made from cloth wrapped in a leather case.

Early twentieth-century handballs were essentially small versions of a football—which allowed them to be gripped and thrown more easily—and consisted of a series of 18 leather panels stitched together and containing an inner bladder inflated via a valve.

The standard 32-panel ball that is still used today was created in the 1950s by Danish company Select. The panels are sewn together using 540 double stitches and 60 corner stitches.

No handball would be complete without hand cream, or more precisely, resin. This is designed to improve the grip and feeling of the ball and ensure a smooth flow between hand and ball.

10

FIELD
HOCKEY

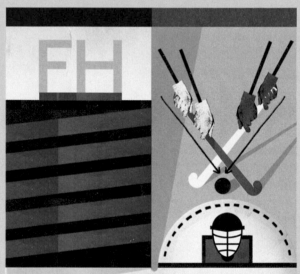

ODD BALLS

The "Indian dribble" is not a problem encountered by masticating infants on the Indian subcontinent, but a revolutionary technique for using a hockey stick, perfected by Indian and Pakistani teams in the 1950s.

Hockey-style games were common throughout Europe in the Middle Ages, going under a variety of names, including cambuca, clubbes, hurl-bat, shinnops, jowling, baddins, bandy ball, and doddorts. Despite sounding like something out of a *Harry Potter* novel, these were, in fact, medieval names for hockey-style games from various parts of England.

The actual word "hockey" may be of Irish origin, although it could also derive from the Anglo-Saxon *hok* for hook, relating to the shape of the stick, or the French *hocquet* for a shepherd's crook.

MYSTERY HISTORY

Hockey is yet another sport that claims to be the world's most popular team game after soccer, which makes it all the more remarkable that so little appears to be known by the game's authorities about the history of their ball. At the time of writing, one of the world's best-known manufacturers of hockey balls didn't even have a website …

That is all the more of a shame since hockey has such a long history—or at least games that are clearly related to it do. Records of curved stick-and-ball games date back at least 4,000 years. Drawings from this period have been found in Egypt; there are depictions of a hockey-like game from 2,500 years ago in Greece, where it was known as Κερητίζειν (pronounced "kerytezin"); Ireland has enjoyed the closely related sport of hurling (see page 78) for at least 2,000 years; and a very similar game from Mongolia, *beikou*, is at least 1,000 years old.

In typical medieval monarch style, cambuca and bandy ball were banned by both Edward III and Richard III in favor of archery practice. But the game prevailed until yet another gaggle of upper-class Brits began to codify it in the late nineteenth century before exporting it around the world, like so many other modern team games.

CUBIST "BALL"

By the 1800s, hockey in England was essentially a public-school game, played with a rubber cube rather than a ball.

Hockey's heartland was south-east England, and the first club in the world was formed in Blackheath, sometime between the late 1840s and 1861. This may have been the handiwork of members of Blackheath Golf Club, which dates back to 1608 and claims to be the world's oldest golf club.

At Blackheath, they also played with a cube of solid rubber, which was designated "not to exceed 7oz [198.5g] in weight" and which frequently had to be boiled to maintain its elasticity.

ROUND IS BETTER

Later clubs included Teddington Cricket Club—the members played hockey as a winter training game—and it was here that, in the first half of the 1870s, someone came up with the spiffing idea of using a ball rather than a glorified dice for the game.

Not surprisingly, the ball they went for was a leather cricket ball, which was painted white but in all other respects was exactly the same as the one they used for their summer game. Even today, hockey balls have the same weight and dimensions as cricket balls.

Not all hockey clubs went along with the innovative idea of using a ball. Even after the Hockey Association was formed in 1886 by seven London clubs, Blackheath refused to join, on the grounds of "our game being so totally at variance with that adopted elsewhere." Blackheath retained their rubber cube along with other arcane additions to their own particular version of the game taken from rugby. These included scrimmaging, catching, and marking.

IN WITH THE NEW

Eventually, Blackheath's idiosyncratic game was elbowed out by what is essentially the modern game, although there have been countless rule changes since the International Rules Board was founded in 1895 (this eventually morphed into the International Hockey Federation).

Hockey quickly spread worldwide, proving especially popular in British colonies. India and Pakistan were powerhouses of the game for many decades. The Indian team was so dominant that it won six consecutive Olympic gold medals between 1928 and 1956, scoring 178 goals and letting in just seven.

The almost universal introduction of synthetic pitches for top-level games in the 1980s was the trigger for not only the decline in Indian hockey dominance, but also the only real change there has been in the hockey ball. Out went the old seamed leather white cricket ball-type ball and in came seamless, plastic balls. These were and are cheaper to produce, more durable, behave more consistently on the playing field, and are not affected by water—this is especially important since synthetic pitches are "water-moderated."

Sansarpur, a small village in India has produced 14 Olympic hockey players—nine of whom share the same surname, Singh.

The ball may be either hollow or have a core, with a plain or dimpled surface. Dimpled balls were developed specifically for use on water-based astroturf surfaces (although they are frequently used on any type of synthetic pitch) to help prevent the hydroplaning that can occur if the ball's outer surface is plain. Dimples also give a more consistent ball speed.

A modern hockey ball has a core made from cork, rubber, injection-molded polyurethane, or, in the case of elite-level balls made by a manufacturer such as Kookaburra, a quilted center.

According to the US Olympic Committee website, field hockey proportionally offers more college scholarships in the US than any other sport, so it definitely pays to play.

A player from the late 1800s would no doubt recognize a modern hockey ball (unless he played for Blackheath) although its response is light years away from that of the heavy old cricket balls of yesteryear.

WE ARE THE CHAMPIONS

The current top sides in world hockey are the Australian men's and the Netherlands women's teams. Both are the current world cup holders—the Aussies have won the trophy three times (one behind Pakistan), while the Dutch women have claimed the title on seven occasions.

II

HURLING

"Teddy McCarthy to John McCarthy, no relation, John McCarthy back to Teddy McCarthy, still no relation."

MÍCHEÁL Ó'MUIRCHEARTAIGH hurling commentator

● ● ● ● ● ● ●

ODD BALLS

The ball used in hurling is known as a *sliotar*, pronounced "slitt-er." The name "hurling" comes from the stick, called a "hurley."

Records show that a form of hurling, which is claimed to be the fastest field sport in the world, has been played in Ireland for 2,000 years.

What was originally a rudimentary stick-and-ball game became, by the eighteenth century, a sport patronized by Anglo-Irish gentry. They had their own teams and played each other regularly.

In 1999 referee Niall Barrett handed out 14 yellow cards and sent off six players in one Irish league game.

The Irish Hurling Union was formed in 1879 to draw up official rules, followed by the Gaelic Athletic Association in 1884.

BROWN MORASS

Early sliotars may have been hollow bronze spheres, leather wrapped around a wooden core, or a tightly bound mix of wood, rope, and animal hair.

Later balls had a solid horsehair core and an outer surface made from two halves of leather stitched together leaving a pronounced seam. These pre-twentieth-century balls tended to soak up water, lose their shape and, being made of brown leather, they often become lost in the muddy brown morass of a winter hurling pitch.

Things did not improve until Johnny McAuliffe of County Limerick made a ball with a cork core and high-quality, two-piece, white-tanned pigskin outer in the early twentieth century. It was lighter than its predecessor, maintained its weight and shape better, had a surer flight, was more visible to players and spectators, and was a forerunner of the modern sliotar.

Today's sliotar is made from a cork core wrapped in threading with a two-part leather cover stitched together on the outside. The pronounced seam remains, a relic of the early designs, because it allows players to catch the ball easily and run with it balanced on the hurley. Even so, modern sliotars are still notorious for variations in shape, weight, water absorbency, and the size of the stitching ridges.

⑫

LACROSSE

> *"I thought lacrosse was what you find in la church."*

ROBIN WILLIAMS actor and comedian. No, it's not very funny but it's the only quote on lacrosse by a famous person

ODD BALLS

The word lacrosse is thought to be derived from the French term for field hockey, *"la jeu de la crosse."*

Lacrosse was a summer Olympic sport in 1904 and 1908—Canada won gold at both events.

A men's lacrosse team has 10 players—three attackers, three midfielders, three defenders, and a goalie.

The rules and field dimensions for women's lacrosse are different from men's. Each team has 12 players, usually four attackers, three midfielders, four defenders, and a goalie.

In the summer of 1763, two Native American tribes played lacrosse to distract British soldiers in order to recapture Fort Michilimackinac in Michigan.

ROLLING STONE

Lacrosse began as a game played by up to 1,000 men over three days on a pitch as much as two miles (3km) long.

At the end of a lacrosse game the winning team gets to keep the ball.

For Native Americans, lacrosse was a celebration of spiritual life and their environment. They played with a ball made from stone, clay, wood, knotted leather strips, or hair-stuffed deerskin.

European settlers took to the game and by 1867 lacrosse had been codified by the founder of Montreal Lacrosse Club, Dr William George Beers.

An indoor version of the game, box lacrosse, was introduced in the 1930s in Canada. Lacrosse is now Canada's official National Summer Sport.

GET A GRIP(PY)

Modern lacrosse balls are solid rubber spheres. They are usually white although a wide range of other colors may be used.

The main manufacturers are the US companies Brine and Warrior. In 2002 Warrior introduced the orange "grippy" ball to Major League Lacrosse to help fans follow the game both live and on TV. The grippy is textured, making it less weather-sensitive than other versions, and giving a better feel for the ball in the stick pocket.

13

LAWN BOWLS

> "I hate middle age.
> Too young for the bowling green,
> too old for Ecstasy."

IAN PATTISON
author, from his successful British sitcom *Rab C. Nesbitt*

EARLY DAYS

There is evidence of people "bowling" rounded rocks at a "peg" as far back as the Stone Age. The ancient Egyptians may have played a game that had similarities to bowls as long ago as 5,000 BC.

Evidence exists of the Romans, Aztecs, ancient Chinese, and Native Americans playing similar games.

Records dating back to the thirteenth century show that an English game known as *jactus lapidum* involved aiming round stones at a target.

ODD BALLS

A few lawn bowls terms:

- Titdwarf: a Bermuda grass hybrid used for the construction of bowling greens

- Singles: a game played between two players

- Jack: the small white ball defined as the target, or mark; also referred to colloquially as the "white," the "kitty," or the "sweetie"

- Kiss: a bowl that glances either the jack or another bowl, resulting in a slight movement of said jack or bowl

- Tickle the kitty: a bowl that moves the jack a slight distance from its current position

- Dumping: a bowl delivered so that it bounces on the turf when it first leaves the hand

- Crack an egg: a description of the weight required to complete an ideal shot

- Drive: a shot where the player delivers the bowl with maximum force toward the target. Known in Scotland as a "blooter"

"It (lawn bowls) has everything. Skill. Guile. Tactics. Uncertainty. Drama. Sledging even. And most importantly, some of the best afternoon tea spreads on offer in Sydney."

GREG GROWDEN reporter on the *Sydney Morning Herald*

Southampton Old Bowling Green on England's south coast hosted its first game in 1299, which makes it the world's oldest bowling green.

In the 1500s ordinary folk were forbidden to play bowls by royal decree—it apparently distracted them from training as soldiers—although the gentry were allowed to play on their own greens, but had to buy a license, which cost £100 a year.

By 1522 "bias," by which a bowl will swing to one side when bowled, had been introduced into the game by Charles Brandon, the Duke of Suffolk.

Bias is produced as a result of the shape of the bowl, although it was originally brought about by inserting weights into one side of the bowl.

LAW OF THE LAWN

The first rules of the game were formulated in 1849 in Glasgow. The Scottish Bowling Association was later formed in 1892 and the English Bowling Association in 1903 under the presidency of famous cricketer Dr W.G. Grace. The world headquarters have remained in Edinburgh.

Lawn bowls has spawned several offshoots, including crown green bowls, short mat bowls (played on a mat 40 to 45ft/12 to 14m in length), indoor bowls, carpet bowls (played on a moveable carpet of 30 x 6ft/9 x 2m), and federation bowls.

BACK TO BOWLS

The term "jack" was introduced in the seventeenth century.

Early bowls were made from *lignum vitae*, a dense, heavy wood (hence the term "woods" to describe them). Some were even made of cast iron. These early wooden bowls were made by hand and so didn't have a consistent shape or weight.

In the nineteenth century, Scottish company Thomas Taylor (still in business today) designed a machine for shaping bowls so they were of a consistent shape and size. Thomas Taylor also made the world's first bias-testing table.

American company Henselite introduced the world's first one-piece, molded, machined, composite plastic bowls in the 1930s. After the war, they followed this with a variety of innovations, including the introduction of dimples for better grip. The Henselite Classic bowl is now the world's most popular bowl.

One side of a bowl features a large symbol within a circle to indicate the side away from the bias. The other side has a small symbol within a circle to indicate the bias side, or the side toward which the bowl will turn when bowled.

In a top-level bowls tournament, competitors may play for up to four hours without a break, walk three to four miles (6.5km), and bend up and down over 100 times.

MARBLES

"I regard golf as an expensive way of playing marbles."

G.K. CHESTERTON writer, poet, journalist, philosopher, and critic

● ● ● ● ● ● ●

ODD BALLS

"**S**unnies" are marbles made of semi-transparent colored glass with small air bubbles within the glass. They're so named because you're supposedly able to observe a solar eclipse through one of them without suffering eye damage.

A marble player's knuckle has to be in touch with the ground when he or she shoots, which is called "knuckling down"—the origin of the phrase "to knuckle down."

"Sporting" marbles can vary in size from ¼in (6mm) to over 3in (76mm) in diameter, and may be made from glass, clay, or agate. Those used in competitions, such as the world championships, must be ¾in (19mm) in diameter for the "shooter" or "tolley" marble and ½in (12.7mm) for the target marble.

FINDING YOUR MARBLES

Hand-made marbles of stone, small rocks, clay, minerals, steel, and glass have been found in societies worldwide, some dating back as far as the ancient Egyptians. Mass-produced ceramic marbles have been around since the 1870s and mass-produced glass marbles since the early twentieth century.

> **Marbles may also be made from marble (of course!), ivory, porcelain, pottery, alabaster, agate, mica, and sulphide. The most popular— glass—have various swirls of color added as the glass cools; or more expensive colored glass may be added to the surface of white or transparent glass.**

BEST IN THE WORLD

The World Marbles Championships take place every year on Good Friday at the Greyhound pub in Tinsley Green, West Sussex, where they have been held since 1932.

The version played is known as Ring Taw, or Ringer in the USA, and involves teams of six attempting to be the first to knock 25 of 49 target marbles out of a 6ft (183cm) diameter ring.

Teams from Britain, Algeria, France, Germany, Netherlands, Estonia, Japan, USA, and Australia have taken part. British teams dominated until the beginning of this century, after which German team 1st MC Erzgebirge has been the outstanding presence in the event.

⓲

PÉTANQUE

"Things got out of hand and I found myself pinned to the wall with a sickle at my throat."

PATRICE JOLIVEAU president of the Pougues-les-Eaux team, in central France, describing an altercation during a game

ODD BALLS

The birthplace of pétanque, La Ciotat, is also famed for the public screening of the world's first movie by the Lumière brothers in September 1895 at the world's first public cinema, L'Eden.

The target ball, or jack, is known correctly as "le bouchon" (the cork), "le but" (the goal), or "le petit" (the little one).

Petanque is played on a "**terrain,**" not a court or pitch.

Pétanque is a type of boules game, and a boules game is one where you throw, or roll, a ball at a small target. Just to confuse things, in the south of France pétanque is commonly known as boules. Other boules games include the Italian bocce and the British lawn bowls (see page 82).

> Most pétanque players refer to playing a game of boules rather than a game of pétanque.

If you win a game 13–0 you are said to "fanny." From this has come the popular image in Provence of a bare-bottomed girl named Fanny whose bum losers must kiss. A substitute picture, carving, or pottery image of a girl's bottom is traditionally provided at pétanque courts for losers to plant a kiss upon.

Competition boules used in pétanque must be made of metal and may bear an engraving of the player's first name, initials, or logo.

"Pointers" (players who throw the boule toward the jack) tend to choose heavier and harder boules, while "shooters" (players who prefer to throw their boule at the opponent's boule to knock it out of play) tend to use lighter and softer boules.

FRENCH THROUGH
AND THROUGH

The name pétanque originates from the Provençal dialect phrase *les peds tanco*, meaning "feet together", which describes the stance when throwing the boule at the jack.

Versions of pétanque have been around for thousands of years. Records exist of similar games being played by the ancient Greeks and Romans and in medieval France. In the Provence region it was known as *jeu provençal*, although in this game players run three steps before delivering the ball; in pétanque they remain stationary. The dimensions and weight of the boules for both games are the same.

ONE BOULE AFTER ANOTHER

Early pétanque-style games used wooden boules which often had iron nails hammered into them to add weight. Later, flathead nails of different colors and materials were used to create remarkably intricate and attractive designs and patterns. As Mike Pegg, former president of the English Pétanque Association and the UK's only international umpire points out: "These boules were larger and heavier then modern boules—from

100 to 150mm [4 to 6in] in diameter and up to 1500g [3¼lb] in weight. The makers became real artists using nails of different metals (steel, brass, and copper) to set out different designs, such as symbols, numbers, and letters, but also stars, flowers, and hearts, according to the wants of the players."

In 1923 Vincent Mille and Paul Courtieu came up with a set of boules made of cast bronze. This was followed five years later by the invention of steel boules by Jean Blanc, a blacksmith from the village of Saint-Bonnet-le-Château, who devised a means of joining the two halves of a boule together.

He sold these from the village ironmongers, and for about 10 years steel boules competed with wooden boules for popularity, eventually taking over in the 1940s as the main type of boule in use.

Today all boules are essentially hollow steel spheres and the majority of manufacturers are based in France, although with the constant spread of the game's appeal, companies in Italy and Thailand have recently been given approval to manufacture competition boules.

16

RUGBY

"I couldn't very well hit him could I? I had the ball in my hands."

TOMMY BISHOP former rugby league player and coach, when questioned about kicking a fellow player

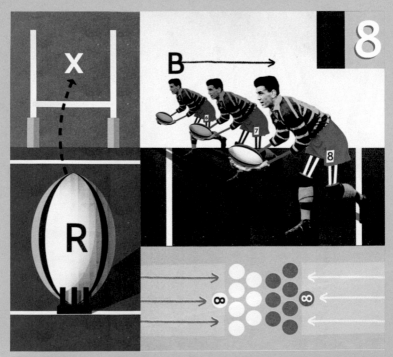

ODD BALLS

The first international rugby union match was between Scotland and England in 1871 at Raeburn Park in Edinburgh. Scotland won 1–0 after William Cross converted a try. Using the present-day scoring system, Scotland would have won 12–5 as they scored two tries and one conversion against England's one try, which they failed to convert.

The reigning Olympic rugby champions are the United States. Rugby Union featured in the Olympics in 1900, 1908, 1920, and 1924. The USA won on the last two occasions and consequently are the most successful Olympic rugby team.

Western Samoa's first international was against Fiji in 1924—there was a tree in the middle of the pitch and the game kicked off at 7 a.m. so the Samoans could go to work afterward.

"Rugby is a game for the mentally deficient ... That is why it was invented by the British. Who else but an Englishman could invent an oval ball?"

PETER COOK English comedian, actor, satirist, and writer

In 2007, an Australian rugby player complained of headaches and lethargy for some weeks after a game. A couple of months later, when he suffered a head injury that required examination, it was discovered he'd had another player's tooth embedded in his skull for all that time ...

The first national anthem sung at a rugby international was on November 16, 1905 when Wales played New Zealand at Cardiff Arms Park. After New Zealand performed the Haka (the Maori's ancestral war dance), the Welsh team responded with *Hen Wlad Fy Nhadau*, and the crowd joined in.

Morley RUFC (rugby union football club) remains a bastion of unionism in Yorkshire, the heartland of rugby league, as a result of the club's two representatives missing the 1895 meeting in Huddersfield, at which the split from union was organized. They decided to stop off for "a drink or two" *en route* to the meeting and consequently missed their train.

A try was so named because it gave the player who scored one the opportunity to try to score a goal by kicking the ball between two posts and over the crossbar, thus converting the try to a goal. The try itself actually earned no points at all.

The Gil Evans whistle is used to start the opening game of every Rugby Union World Cup. It was first used by Welsh referee Gil Evans in the match between England and New Zealand in 1905, and it was also used at the kick-off of the final of the 1924 Paris Olympics.

RUNNING WITH THE BALL

The invention of rugby is credited to William Webb Ellis of Rugby School in Warwickshire in 1823. A form of football in which the hands were used had been played at the school since 1750, but Webb Ellis took it further. He was accused of cheating, and consequently "held in low regard."

In the Roman game of *harpastum* both hands and feet were used, and games such as "cnapan" in Pembrokeshire, Wales, "campball" in eastern England, "hurling to goales" in Cornwall, southwest England, and the "Atherstone Ball Game", Warwickshire, all date from medieval times and have similarities to modern-day rugby.

By 1845, Rugby School had developed rules for the game—prior to this, 300 or more players would take part in a school match— and the first balls made specifically for the sport were constructed in 1832 by William Gilbert (1799–1877). He was shoemaker to Rugby School and, in 1842, moved to premises directly opposite the school's playing field.

INFLATED BLADDERS

Early games used a bladder filled with paper or straw and no two balls were ever the same shape, size, or weight. Later balls were made from four pieces of cowhide stitched together and inflated by a pig's bladder, which gave the "prolate sphere" shape. The bladder, still green and smelly, was inflated through the stem of a clay pipe.

According to E.F.T. Bennett, who played for Rugby School in the mid-1800s, "The shape of our ball came from the bladder and was a perfect ball for long drop kicking or placing and for dribbling too ..."

In 1870, Richard Lindop, a former pupil at Rugby School, invented an inflatable rubber bladder, which was both easier to blow up and helped prevent illnesses caused through inflating a raw pig's bladder by lung power.

In the late nineteenth century, a ball inflator was invented, based on an enlarged ear syringe.

In 1871 William Gilbert's nephew James Gilbert exhibited the Rugby School Football at the Great Exhibition in London under "Educational Appliances" and went on to export rugby balls to British colonies, including Australia, New Zealand, and South Africa.

BALL INNOVATIONS

The Rugby Football Union (RFU) was founded in 1871, and in 1892 it introduced standard dimensions for the ball. Four panels became the official construction technique. Prior to this six and eight-panel balls were also produced.

Materials for the ball's outer covering included camel hide and pigskin as well as cowhide. The first two were easier to work with but were not popular with players since they were slippery when wet.

Henry Timms, who made some 50,000 balls for Gilbert between 1890 and 1935, introduced the technique of dry-leather stitching. Balls no longer had to be made up wet and dried out before being dispatched to market.

TWO CAN PLAY AT THAT GAME

In 1895, rugby split into two codes, union and league. This came about mainly as a result of the RFU enforcing amateurism on the game— a harsh imposition on the working-class northern clubs, whose players relied heavily on "broken-time payments" in order to take time off work to play the game.

There is very little difference between the balls used by union and league. Rugby League balls are a bit smaller and traditionally have six panels as this gives a more pointy shape, which is better for kicking, although today four-panel balls are increasingly common. The balls may be similar but to quote Tony Collins, professor of the social history of sport at Leeds Metropolitan University, "The only thing the two sports really have in common is the shape of the posts and the balls."

NEW BALLS

The dimensions of the union ball were reduced by an inch (2.5cm) and the weight raised by 1.45oz (41g) in 1932 to make it better for handling, although different nations had their own design preferences. The Kiwis and Aussies preferred torpedo-shaped balls, South Africans went for eight panels for better grip, and the UK nations stayed with four panels.

Gilbert remained the main manufacturer for both union and league balls up to the 1970s. Gilbert Match, made from cowhide, was the standard issue for union internationals in 1960. For a while, Gilbert remained with natural leather as other companies moved on to various synthetics and laminates that reduced water retention and allowed better handling.

Companies such as Webb Ellis, and in rugby league, Steeden from Australia, are the other major players in the market today.

Gilbert still provides the official Rugby Union World Cup ball in the form of the Gilbert Match XV, a synthetic and laminate structure, which uses a patented Multi-Matrix pimple pattern for better handling. Star-shaped and round pimples had been used before this, again on synthetic rather than leather surfaces.

In Australia, Steeden's name is often used generically for a rugby league ball.

A modern rugby ball from either code is a complex composite of modern materials technology, using computational fluid dynamics analysis, nanotechnology, and 3D modeling to determine the optimum shape and placement of the pimples for minimum drag and maximum travel. All a far cry from a straw-filled bladder …

HIGH SCORES

The highest scoring game in the Rugby Union World Cup was when New Zealand beat Japan 145–17 on June 4, 1995.

The highest score in an international rugby league match is France's 120–0 defeat of Serbia and Montenegro in the Mediterranean Cup played in Beirut, Lebanon on October 22, 2003.

The highest score ever was recorded on February 8, 2015 in Belgium when Royal Kituro beat Soignies 356–3. Kituro ran in 56 tries, meaning they crossed the line roughly every 90 seconds.

SHOT PUT

> **"** Some kinda greenish powder
> came out of it. **"**

RANDY BARNES
world record holder, describing his favorite shot splitting open

ODD BALLS

Shot putting has its origins in nineteenth-century Scottish Highland Games. The shot was a stone or metal sphere of varying size thrown from behind a line. Weights varied from 16 to 26lb (7.25 to 11.75kg).

The word "shot" is derived from the shot used in warfare. Stone or metal shots were sometimes used instead of cannonballs. "Put" derives from an old Scottish term for "thrust" and refers to the throwing action of a shot putter.

"Putting the weight," as shot putting was originally known in the Highland Games, mixes both Scottish and English terminology since a "weight" is an old English measure equal to 16lb (7.25kg), the same weight as the men's shot put in modern track and field events.

Old shots were often made from stone. Modern shots
are made from cast iron or brass. Those for indoor
meets consist of a plastic shell filled with
fine lead shot.

TECHNIQUE IS ALL

Shot-putting techniques use one of three styles: the
glide, the spin, and the cartwheel (not literally!).

- The glide originated in the USA in 1951, when Parry O'Brien
  developed a technique that involved facing backward in the
  circle, thrusting off from one leg to turn 180 degrees in a
  gliding motion before launching the shot.
- For the spin, developed by Brian Oldfield in the 1970s, the
  thrower faces the rear of the circle and spins around on the
  ball of one foot before placing the opposite foot in the center
  of the circle. The thrower spins on this, places the first foot
  down toward the front of the circle, and while facing forward,
  launches the shot.
- The cartwheel also involves starting the throw facing the rear
  of the circle and some quite athletic leaping around from one
  leg to the other before launching the shot.

**Professional male shot putters tend to favor the
spin. The glide is more popular at amateur level
and among women, but the cartwheel has gained
favor in women's shot putting in recent years.**

A shot putter must enter and leave the 7ft (2m)
diameter throwing circle from its rear half,
otherwise a foul throw will be called.

SOFTBALL

"If history repeats itself, I should think we can expect the same thing again."

TV COMMENTATOR Beijing Olympics softball competition, 2008

ODD BALLS

In October 2008 softball players in Kissimmee, Florida, had to rescue the pilot of a small plane who crashed after clipping the goalpost of a nearby football field on take off.

The official color for most softballs is yellow, although traditional white balls are also allowed, especially in the slow-pitch game.

Softball has also been known as kitten ball, diamond ball, cabbage ball, and pumpkin ball.

In Chicago it's common to play with an old-fashioned 16in (40.5cm) ball, which is softer than the standard 12in (30.5cm) ball and sometimes called a mush ball.

PLAYGROUND FUN

Disintegrating balls were an early problem in softball, so much so that sporting goods manufacturer A.G. Spalding were asked for help. They developed a ball smaller than an indoor baseball but bigger than a regular baseball. These "playground" balls were made with an elkhide cover. Raised seams protected the stitching from being worn away by the bat and the playing surface, and they were soft enough to be fielded without using a glove.

Walter Hakanson of the YMCA eventually came up with the official name "softball" at a 1926 meeting of the US National Recreation Congress. By 1934 the name was standardized throughout the country, as were the rules, and internationally the USA remains the number-one player of softball.

The ball has not changed much since the 1930s. Up to 2002 it was usually made up of two pieces of white leather or synthetic material in the shape of a figure of eight, sewn together with red thread. After that, the white leather was replaced by high-visibility yellow casings. The core may be made of long-fiber kapok, a mixture of cork and rubber, or a polyurethane mixture.

There are at least three different versions of how softball was invented …

- Thanksgiving Day 1887, Chicago, and alumni of Yale and Harvard universities begin knocking a boxing glove back and forth with a broom handle after an annual football match between them at the Farragut Boat Club. From this, two years later, George Hancock developed a proper bat and ball and the Farragut Club came up with rules for a game known as indoor baseball, using a 16in (40.5cm) diameter ball.

- A few years after this, firemen in Minneapolis were playing a similar game, kitten ball, invented by Lewis Rober Sr as an outdoor exercise for the fire crews. It used a 12in (30.5cm) diameter ball and had a different-sized diamond from the one used in Chicago (softball eventually combined the Minneapolis ball and the Chicago diamond).

- In 1916, employees of the Atchison, Topeka, and Santa Fe Railway in Kansas started to play a version of indoor baseball using a ball of only 5½–6in (14–15.25cm) diameter, which was so soft it was regularly smashed to pieces by the bat.

19

SQUASH

"Squash—that's not exercise, it's flagellation."

NOËL COWARD writer, actor, and singer, known for his wit and flamboyance

ODD BALLS

Early squash balls were a different size in the UK and the USA. One reason for this is said to be that a British squash official traveling to the USA with the "correct" dimensions for the ball happened to be aboard the *Titanic* and consequently never made it …

The world-record speed for hitting a squash ball is 176 mph (283.25 km/h), which was achieved by Australian Cameron Pilley on May 9, 2014.

Squash is one of the best cardiovascular workouts you can get—in a one-hour game a decent player may burn between 700 and 1,000 calories.

The Avon India Rubber Company produced a squash ball in the 1920s that had a hole in it and was known as the Bath Club Holer.

SQUASHED BALL, NEW GAME

S quash began its journey to worldwide popularity at Harrow School in the nineteenth century when pupils playing rackets and fives, both of which involve using a racket to whack a small hollow rubber ball against the sides of a four-walled-court, noticed that when the ball was punctured it allowed them to play a wider variety of shots.

Playing with a "squashed" ball took off, and squash soon became popular in other British public schools and universities, so that by 1908 a committee had been set up to organize the sport.

Up until the 1920s there was wide variation in the size, weight, and composition of squash balls. They were universally made from rubber, but, for example, the Avon India Rubber Company produced balls varying from 1.5in (3.8cm) to 1.7in (4.3cm) in diameter with finishes that could be matt or varnished.

A member of the Royal Automobile Club in London, Col R.E. Crompton, managed to get his club's standard ball adopted for amateur championships after he spent time weighing, measuring, and comparing the bounce of various different squash balls.

Details on the ball, which was produced by the Silvertown Company and known as the Wisden Royal, were lost in a fire at the factory in World War Two, but it was given a run for its money by two additional balls, both produced by the India Rubber and Gutta Percha Company, which were 3 percent and 5 percent slower respectively.

MAINTAINING STANDARDS

By 1926 the Tennis and Rackets Association had laid down exact specifications for squash balls to be used for competition play, marked 'T and RA – Standard' in red lettering. They were produced by both Gradidge and Silvertown. By 1928 the Silvertown ball was used exclusively for championship games.

World War Two marked the end of Silvertown as a major player on the squash scene. (It was difficult even to get new squash balls due to the scarcity of rubber and the bombing of major ball producers' factories.) After the war, Dunlop became the major manufacturer, followed by Slazenger in the sixties.

Slazenger produced the first synthetic ball from butyl, a synthetic rubber that is not so affected by the temperature of the court as the real thing, although it was not as resilient as rubber and balls would frequently split during a game.

In the early seventies, Dunlop introduced the colored dot on balls to mark their speed. Their balls, arguably the most popular, are made from Malaysian rubber mixed with up to 15 different ingredients to produce the correct consistency for the particular speed of ball being made.

TYPES OF SQUASH BALL

Color	Speed	Bounce
double yellow dot	extra super slow	very low
yellow dot	super slow	low
green or white dot	slow	average
red dot	medium	high
blue dot	fast	very high

The Women's Squash Rackets Association was formed in 1934, and chose the Gradidge ball for their competitions.

"If you think squash is a competitive activity, try flower arranging."

ALAN BENNETT writer and actor

ROUGH HANDLING

Basically, squash balls are made from two halves of rubber compound, glued together to form a hollow sphere then buffed to a matt finish.

The balls undergo a rigorous testing process, which includes being compressed between two metal plates and pulled apart until the seam breaks.

The bounciness of a squash ball depends on the resilience of the rubber it is made from. This is affected by all manner of things, not least of which is the fact that as the ball is smashed against the court walls, the air inside becomes pressurized, which leads to the rubber becoming more resilient and the ball bouncing more.

The choice of competition balls depended on the size of the court. Once this was standardized, the balls were standardized, too.

In a game, the ball will heat up to around 113°F (45°C), when equilibrium is reached and it plays at its best.

In the longest-ever squash rally Jahangir Khan (Pakistan) and Gamal Awad (Egypt) kept it going for seven minutes. Leo Au (Hong Kong) and Shawn Delierre (Canada) played the longest-ever game at the Holtrand Gas City Pro-Am 2015 in Canada. It lasted for 2 hours 50 minutes.

TABLE TENNIS

"Ping pong is coming home."

BORIS JOHNSON the Mayor of London at the 2008 Beijing Olympics, during handover ceremony to London for the 2012 games

ODD BALLS

Table tennis was once banned in the Soviet Union because it was thought to be harmful to the eyes.

How many balls can two players hit back and forth in 60 seconds? The current record is 173, set by Jackie Bellinger and Lisa Lomas in 1993.

Table tennis paddles or bats are correctly known as rackets according to the International Table Tennis Federation (ITTF).

The choice of color of the ball is made according to the table color and its surroundings—a white ball is easier to see on a green or blue table than it is on a gray table.

Table-tennis aficionados claim it is the most popular racket sport in the world and the second most played sport overall.

ANYONE FOR TABLE TENNIS?

The first table-tennis "balls" were made from the top of a Champagne cork or a rolled-up ball of string and were a feature of English parlor games in the 1880s. A line of books across a dining table made up the "net" and a cigar-box lid or book served as the "racket."

Table tennis has also been known as ping pong, whiff waff, pom pom, netto, and tennis de salon.

The first "Table Tennis" game was a board-and-dice game made in 1887 by J.H. Singer of New York and based on lawn tennis. In 1890 English company David Foster produced a miniature version of tennis as a table-top parlor game, featuring a 1in (30mm) cloth-covered rubber ball and strung rackets.

In 1898 London manufacturer John Jaques devised a new game called Gossima, which used rackets, a 2in (50mm) web-wrapped cork ball and a 12in (30cm) high net. This was renamed "Gossima or Ping-Pong" in 1900—the last part of the name was derived from the sound the ball made on the rackets, which is not at all similar to the sound made by modern equipment.

Eventually, Hamleys of London trademarked the name "ping-pong" and sold it to Parker Brothers in the USA.

BOUNCY BOUNCY

Most nineteenth-century balls were poor—rubber balls bounced too much, cork balls not enough—but on a trip to the USA in 1901, English table-tennis enthusiast James Gibb came across celluloid balls, which had just the right bounce. So the table-tennis ball became a hollow, celluloid, gas-filled sphere with a matt finish (usually white or orange), which could be produced so inexpensively that being easily damaged was not an issue. And so it remained, more or less, until 2014.

For competition, 1½in (38mm) balls were used until 2000, when fractionally larger balls were introduced to make them easier for spectators to see, particularly on TV, since even that tiny increase in diameter slowed the balls down.

Two players at the 1936 world championships in Prague took more than two hours to contest a single point.

In July 2014, the ITTF decreed that balls for international tournaments must be made from plastic as opposed to celluloid—this was mainly because of health issues with the manufacture of celluloid balls (celluloid is a hazardous substance). "Poly" balls have been phased in over two years, and are slightly bigger than the celluloid balls.

Ping-pong ball grading varies from zero to three stars. A no-star ball is for kids, novices, and training. One and two-star balls are used in schools, youth clubs, and by improving players. Three-star balls are favored for competitions due to their consistent roundness, balance, and bounce.

As of June 2016, there were 77 table-tennis balls approved by the ITTF.

E.C. Goode made the first table-tennis racket
with a sheet of pimpled rubber
glued to a wooden blade in 1901.

SPEEDY SPINNING

Spin is a vital component of table tennis, and
is achieved largely due to the composition of
the rubber covering of the racket. Sponge rubber/
reversed sponge rubber covers were introduced
in the 1950s.

The fastest
recorded smash,
by New Zealander
Lark Brandt,
reached 70 mph
(112.5 km/h).

The small size and low density
of a ping-pong ball creates
a whirlpool of rotating air
or liquid about itself, which
helps to produce the various
types of spin that are integral
to the game.

Modern rackets have a combination of a thin layer of
rubber with inward- or outward-pointing pimples on
top of a sponge rubber layer, all laid atop a plywood/
carbon/synthetic core. This construction helps to
maximize the spin and speed of the ball.

**A decent player takes around
0.25 seconds to react to
a shot, while a world-class
player takes 0.18 seconds
or even less.**

Table tennis was the
inspiration for the
first commercially
successful video
game, Atari's "Pong"
in the 1970s.

21

TENNIS

> "Tennis is a perfect combination of violent action taking place in an atmosphere of total tranquility."

BILLIE JEAN KING former world number one, founder of the Women's Tennis Association, World Team Tennis, and the Women's Sports Foundation

ODD BALLS

A tennis ball's coefficient of drag is calculated thus: $C_o = D/0.5 \, q \, u2 \, A$ where D is the drag force, q is the density of air (1.21 kg/m2), u is the velocity of the ball relative to the fluid, and A the cross-sectional area.

The fuzzy surface of the felt is a vital component in how tennis balls travel through the air. It enables players to impart spin to the ball, since it creates air drag and friction, which allows backspin and topspin. Scientific papers have been written on the subject, and the ITF (International Tennis Federation) have tested tennis balls in wind tunnels and have a special rig designed to test ball spin with different rackets. Even NASA has studied the aerodynamics of tennis balls.

> # "I love Wimbledon. But why don't they stage it in the summer?"
>
> **VIJAY AMRITRAJ** former tennis professional discussing the sodden 2007 Wimbledon Championships

Two possible origins of the word "tennis":

- From the French *tenez*, which means "take it/ take that." This may have been shouted upon serving the ball in early games.

- From the game's possible—but very speculative— origins in Tinnis, an Egyptian town on the banks of the Nile.

The service was apparently invented by Henry VIII, who had servants throw the ball up for him to strike as he was too fat to do it himself.

The longest match on record took place in 2010 at Wimbledon, when John Isner (USA) and Nicolas Mahut (France) played for 11 hours 5 minutes over three days in a game that Isner eventually won 6–4, 3–6, 6–7 (7), 7–6 (3), 70–68.

The shortest match on record is the 1922 Wimbledon final, where Suzanne Lenglen beat Molla Mallory in 23 minutes.

The use of "love" for zero is shrouded in mystery. One origin is said to be from the French word *l'oeuf* as in "egg," meaning zero.

The official world record speed for a tennis serve is held by Samuel Groth of Australia—163.4 mph (263 km/h) at the Busan Open 2012 Challenger Event. However, there is evidence (though often disputed) that Big Bill Tilden (USA) clocked up 163.6 mph (263.3 km/h) way back in 1931.

The tennis grounds at Wimbledon are owned by All England Lawn Tennis Ground plc and consist of 19 grass courts (including Center Court and No.1 Court), eight American Clay courts, and five indoor courts (two Greenset Velvelux and three Greenset Trophy).

ECCLESIASTICAL TO REGAL PURSUIT

The first accounts of a game approximating to modern tennis originate in eleventh-century France, where monks knocked a crudely fashioned ball back and forth by hand over a rope stretched across a monastery quadrangle.

It was known as *jeu de paume*, due to the use of the palms. Around the twelfth century leather gloves were introduced, then in the sixteenth century short rackets—probably due to the fact that early tennis balls were made from leather stuffed with wool or horsehair and were hard on the palm of the hand.

By this time, the game had evolved into an indoor game, popular among French and British royalty and aristocracy, hence the term "court" for the playing area. This version of the game is still played and is known as Real or Court Tennis.

By the eighteenth century, the ball was made from thin strips of wool wound tightly around an inner core, which was then tied up with string. The whole lot was stitched inside a white cloth outer layer.

Major Walter Clopton Wingfield brought out two books on tennis, *The Book of the Game* (1873) and *The Major's Game of Lawn Tennis* (1874).

TENNIS MOVES OUTSIDE

Tennis as we know it today took off in Victorian times. In 1872 the world's first tennis club was formed in Leamington Spa, based on a game devised by Major Harry Gem and Augurio Pereira, while the following year Major Walter Clopton Wingfield brought out a very similar game called *sphairistike* (from the Greek σφάίρίστική, meaning "skill at playing at ball") or lawn tennis. This was based on the old game played by royalty and used much of the French terminology of the original sport.

"To be a tennis champion, you have to be inflexible. You have to be stubborn. You have to be arrogant. You have to be selfish and self-absorbed."

CHRIS EVERT former world number one and president of the Women's Tennis Association

At the first Wimbledon Championships, held in 1877, the balls consisted of solid India rubber spheres, although it was soon found that they lasted longer and were better to play with if flannel was stitched on top of the rubber.

The flannel was eventually replaced by hard-wearing Melton cloth, a tight-woven woollen cloth that originated in Melton Mowbray in Leicestershire. This felt fabric is still used today, along with Needle cloth, which is less hard-wearing.

According to the official Wimbledon website, 54,250 balls are used during the Championship. Around 20,000 are allocated for practice purposes and the rest are used on court. During a match, an umpire will request that all balls are changed after seven games are played and then after every nine games.

FEEL THE PRESSURE

Eventually, a hollow rubber sphere was introduced, which was cut to shape using "clover leaf" segments. The ball was filled with pressurizing gases, which were activated as the core was molded by heat into a spherical shape.

Later balls have two separate rubber hemispheres joined together under pressure to give a uniform shape and predictable response.

The felt fabric used on a modern tennis ball is woven using cotton and a wool/nylon mix, after which it's dyed and finished. Then two "dogbones" of fabric are cut, after application of a latex backing, and stuck to the latex-covered core. The ball is cured and tumbled slowly through a steam-laden atmosphere, which causes the cloth to fluff, giving a soft, raised surface. The ridge where the two halves of the ball are cemented together disappears.

The seam on a tennis ball is actually the glue that has come up through the two pieces of felt that make up the surface of the ball.

Logos are applied before the balls are packed in pressurized cans. Balls lose their pressure about a month after opening the can. However, not all tennis balls are pressurized—you can buy pressureless balls with a solid core. These are used mainly for training. They don't lose their bounce as pressurized balls do, although the felt will wear off eventually.

PLENTY OF CHOICE

The ITF introduced yellow balls in 1972 (Wimbledon held off until 1986) because they are easier for TV viewers to see. Up until then tennis balls were white, or occasionally black, depending on the background color of the court.

Just one type of tennis ball was used in competition play until 1989 when high-altitude balls were introduced to allow for different atmospheric pressure. Then in 2002, Types 1, 2, and 3 balls became available—Type 1 for slower courts, 2 for standard courts, and 3 for fast courts.

Tennis balls vary slightly, depending on the manufacturer and model, and experienced players can instantly tell the difference between balls—they may feel lighter or heavier, harder or softer, more or less bouncy, have a coarser or finer cover, and require varying degrees of effort in order to generate the same speed.

22
TEN-PIN BOWLING

"There's kind of a Zen aspect to bowling. The pins are either staying up or down before you even throw your arm back."

JEFF BRIDGES actor and star of bowling movie *The Big Lebowski*

ODD BALLS

The largest bowling alley in the world is Inazawa Grand Bowling Center in Japan, with 116 lanes.

The average speed of a bowling ball moving down the alley is 17–19 mph (27–31 km/h).

There are estimated to be over 100 million bowlers worldwide, making ten-pin bowling one of the world's most popular sports.

Henry VIII used cannonballs for bowling.

SCATTERING SKITTLES

The first game involving knocking down pins or skittles dates back over 5,000 years to ancient Egypt.

The first written record of the game comes from 1366 when Edward III banned bowling in England as it was a distraction from training for warfare.

Meanwhile, in Germany a game called *kegel* involved bowling at nine skittles. This, along with English and Dutch versions of bowling, was introduced to America during the colonial era. There is evidence of a ten-pin game being played in Britain in the early nineteenth century.

Ten-pin bowling became popular in the USA after nine-pin bowling was banned in 1841, owing to its links with organized gambling. By this time, the first indoor bowling alley had opened in New York.

BALL TALK

The balls used in New York's first indoor bowling alley were made from a heavy wood known as *lignum vitae*, which is so dense that it will sink in water.

In 1905 the first rubber bowling ball was produced, and in 1914 Brunswick began to manufacture balls made from Mineralite, a hard rubber compound.

In the US, over 20,000 people a year end up in hospital following a trip to the bowling alley.

Maude Lebowski: "What do you do
for recreation?"
The Dude: "Oh, the usual. I bowl. Drive
around. The occasional acid flashback."

JEFF BRIDGES as the Dude in *The Big Lebowski*

In the 1970s, polyester balls were introduced, early versions of which sometimes became lopsided. This was followed by Ebonite's first polyurethane ball in 1981, which had better grip on wooden lane surfaces.

In the early 1990s, Nu-Line developed the reactive resin surface, which is common on modern balls. Since this time, developments in bowling balls have been so rapid that it's been almost impossible for the rules of the game to keep up.

Technology has allowed balls to become increasingly flamboyant, with surfaces featuring everything from multiple and iridescent colors to designs that appear to have objects embedded within the ball.

DELVING DEEP

The design of the ball's core has undergone huge changes. Prior to the 1990s it was basically a heavy sphere inside the ball. After about 1990, computer-designed core shapes were introduced for different weights of ball, and extra weights and counterweights were either added to the core or placed elsewhere inside the ball.

This is important because the purpose of the core is to stabilize the rolling ball. Cores consist of various materials, including dense plastic, ceramics, or a resin/graphite mix. Iron oxide or zirconium may be used for counterweights.

Once these changes to the core were made, "perfect games" (12 successive throws in which all 10 pins are knocked over) became increasingly common, leading to the argument that using modern balls requires less skill from the bowler. Complex "dynamic balance" regulations were therefore introduced to help offset this.

GETTING TO GRIPS

There are two different types of bowling grip—conventional and finger-tip. In a conventional grip, the bowler's ring and middle fingers are placed into the ball up to the second joint. In a finger-tip grip, the ring and middle fingers are inserted into the ball up to the first joint. More strength is needed for the finger-tip grip but it gives the bowler better control in rotating the ball.

The three finger holes affect the behavior of the ball since they affect core dynamics. They are drilled into the ball after manufacture to suit the bowler's hand, with a hole each for the thumb, ring finger, and middle finger, although up to five holes are allowed. Customized balls may allow the bowler to use a ball that is a pound or two (around a kilo) heavier than a standard model.

The bowling lane has a huge effect on how a ball and bowler perform. Wooden bowling lanes are "oiled" on a regular basis. The first two-thirds of the lane receive the heaviest application of oil, which results in the ball first sliding (as opposed to rolling) and then spinning and curving when it hits the drier, less well-oiled end. This, plus the way the ball rotates and the effect of individual delivery style, is taken into account by top players.

23

VOLLEYBALL

ODD BALLS

The Beatles played a match on Sorrento Beach in Los Angeles in the early 1960s, watched by President John F. Kennedy.

Indian female beach volleyball players refused to wear bikinis in the 2008 World Beach Volleyball tournament.

The fastest recorded spike is 82 mph (132 km/h) by Bulgarian outside hitter Matey Kaziyski.

> "I used to go over to
> Gene Kelly's house and play
> volleyball, and Paul Newman and
> Marlon Brando were
> always there."

JOAN COLLINS actress and author

The longest recorded volleyball marathon between two teams of six is 75 hours 30 minutes at Kingston, North Carolina in 1980.

NO TOUCHING

Volleyball is derived from a game known as *mintonette*, which was invented on February 9, 1895 in Holyoke, Massachusetts by one William G. Morgan, a YMCA physical education director.

Most volleyball players jump about 300 times during a match.

Morgan wanted an alternative to basketball for older YMCA members, which involved less physical contact, so he took component parts of handball (hitting the ball) and tennis (the net) to make up his new game.

Sports ball manufacturer Spalding was contracted to make a ball for this new game, which became known as volleyball after the name was put forward by Alfred Halstead at an exhibition match in 1896.

Spalding's new ball had a rubber bladder and was the same size and weight as a modern volleyball. Indeed, there have been no changes to the dimensions since the earliest days of the game, and the design has remained much the same—18 rectangular panels of leather or synthetic material wrapped around a bladder, with a valve to regulate internal air pressure. The panels are arranged in six identical sections of three panels each.

BIGGER AND BRIGHTER

Beach volleyballs are slightly larger than regular volleyballs despite weighing the same, and have a rougher surface and a lower internal pressure, which makes them softer.

Generally, beach volleyballs tend to be more brightly colored than regular volleyballs, but those used to play the indoor game can come in three distinct colors as well as plain white.

IN GOOD COMPANY

Spalding's grip on the volleyball market was long ago broken by several other manufacturers, particularly those from Japan. In 1952, Tachikara produced a revolutionary seamless ball—referred to these days as a molded or laminated ball—in place of traditional asymmetrical hand-stitched balls. This improved the ball's shape, air retention, rebound, and overall durability.

Later developments by Tachikara include its patented Loose Bladder Construction (LBC) method, introduced in 1964, when volleyball made its debut at the Olympic Games in Tokyo. This allows a layer of air to circulate between the inside bladder and a cotton canvas/leather outside cover, resulting in a truer flight and a superior soft touch.

Tachikara's Dual Bladder Construction (DBC) volleyball appeared in 2003, featuring two internal, independent bladders. An impact-reducing layer of air circulates between the two, resulting in a ball that is theoretically twice as durable and responsive and has improved control and flight.

The official indoor and beach volleyballs of the Fédération Internationale de Volleyball (FIVB) are produced by Mikasa, a company with Japanese origins, now based in the USA.

Molten, also Japanese, have the top-of-the-range FLISTATEC. This is made from an outer layer of microfiber-based synthetic leather, which is as soft as natural leather and absorbs perspiration as well, but retains a dry surface better. Inside this is a rubber cover, which helps to improve durability and creates a better feel. This in turn contains a butyl bladder to prevent air leaking out.

ACKNOWLEDGMENTS

The author would like to thank the team at Dog 'n' Bone for taking on this project.

The publisher would like to thank Blair Frame for his illustrations and Jerry Goldie for the design.

ABOUT THE AUTHOR

Alf Alderson is an award-winning adventure sports and travel journalist and photographer based in Pembrokeshire, south-west Wales. His writing has appeared in a wide range of publications and websites including *The Guardian, Daily Telegraph, Independent, Toronto Globe & Mail, South China Morning Post, Financial Times,* and *Mpora.* When he can be bothered, Alf occasionally posts scurrilous comments on his own blog, alfalderson.co.uk/blog, and also tweets as @alfinwales.